# HISTORY OF
# FOOD AND COOKING

## RICHARD WOOD

**WAYLAND**

# Books in the series
History of Canals
History of Fairs and Markets
History of Food and Cooking
History of Toys and Games

**Series editor:** Sarah Doughty
**Book editor:** Ruth Raudsepp
**Designer:** Michael Leaman
**Production controller:** Carol Stevens

First published in 1996 by Wayland (Publishers) Limited
61 Western Road, Hove, East Sussex BN3 1JD, England.

**British Library Cataloguing in Publication Data**
**Wood, Richard**
**History of Food and Cooking. – (History of Series)**
**I. Title II. Series**
**641. 3009**

ISBN 0-7502-1681-6

Picture Acknowledgements
CM Dixon 9, 10, 13 (top & bottom), 14, 15 (bottom); Corinium Museum 11,
Hulton Deutsch Collection 22 (top & bottom), 30, 33 (top & bottom), 35, 39, 41, 42, 43;
Mary Evans Picture Library 20, 34 (top & bottom); Michael Holford 6, 7 (top), 8, 27, 29;
National Trust Photographic Library 24 (bottom), 32; Norfolk Museums Service 7; Richard Wood 24 (top), 28 (bottom);
Robert Harding Picture Library 12, 15 (top), 16 (top); Sainsbury's 38 (bottom);
The Bridgeman Art Library 5, 17, 18, 20 (top), 21, 25, 26, 28 (top), 31, 36 (bottom), 37.
The remaining pictures are from the Wayland Picture Library.

Typeset by Michael Leaman Design Partnership
Printed and bound in England
by B. P. C. Paulton Books

# Contents

Words that are printed in **bold** in the text are explained in the glossary on page 46.

# Introduction

Throughout history, many people have had very little food to eat. It was only the rich who could afford luxuries like spices or **exotic** fruits from abroad. Before railways and roads were built most food was grown very close to where it was eaten. The quantities and types of food people ate changed according to the season of the year and the weather. A good harvest would mean plenty of food, but a poor harvest meant that most people had little to eat. The type of landscape and climate also had an effect on the kinds of food that could be grown. Until the nineteenth century, bread made with wheat flour was more common in the south of Britain, but in the north of the country and in Scotland, people grew rye and ate oat cakes and porridge because wheat would not grow well there.

▼ *Fast food like pizza comes ready-prepared from take-away food shops.*

## Our Daily Bread

In Britain today, every year we eat on average, 60 kg of bread and rice, 70 kg of meat and fish, 165 kg of fruit and vegetables and at least 12 kg of sugar. Our ancestors would be surprised at the many types of food we have to choose from and the amount of food we eat. They would not recognize some foods, such as potatoes and tomatoes, because these were not widely eaten before about 1750. However, perhaps they would be most amazed by the way we use packets and tins to keep our food fresh. Tinned and frozen foods were unheard of until the nineteenth century, and pre-cooked foods and ready-to-eat meals did not appear in the supermarkets until the 1970s and 1980s.

## Kitchen Bliss

Our ancestors would have welcomed our kitchens containing clean and easy-to-use gas or electric cookers and microwaves. Preparing and cooking food in iron cauldrons hung above log fires was hard and very hot work. Through the centuries, people have seen many changes in food and cooking. This book looks at the way food and cooking has changed and developed from prehistoric times to the present day.

▲ *There were cook shops and pie shops that sold cooked meats in* **medieval** *towns, but much food was made at home. This 500-year-old picture shows cheese being made by hand in the home.*

◀ *In medieval times most people worked on the land to produce enough food to eat. This calendar shows some of the jobs done each month.*

# Prehistoric Food

### From Hunters to Farmers

The first people to live in Britain were **nomadic** hunters who, came from mainland Europe about 300,000 years ago. **Archaeologists** have learnt a great deal about the food these people ate from studying their bones and the things they made. **Prehistoric** people lived mainly on plants they could gather and animals they could hunt. It was not until about 3,500 BC that people in Britain began to farm the land by growing crops and keeping domestic animals such as cattle and sheep.

▲ *A 10,000-year-old cave painting of a bison. **Stone Age** people hunted bison for food.*

### Hunters and Gatherers

The types of wild animal that roamed across Britain changed with the climate. During cold periods such as the great Ice Age, which ended about 10,000 BC, now-extinct animals such as woolly mammoth (a type of elephant), bison (a type of buffalo) and reindeer were common. During warmer periods, these were replaced by elephants, deer and wild oxen. During the Ice Age, Britain was still joined to mainland Europe. Bones and paintings, such as those discovered in caves in the Ardèche region of France, suggest that these animals were hunted for food. Families of hunters lived a nomadic life and they followed the herds of animals wherever they went to be sure of a ready supply of food. A mammoth or bison might be chased into a pit, and while trapped would be killed with stone-tipped spears.

Today, hunting communities in other parts of the world get most of their food from plants rather than animals. This was probably true in prehistoric times too. Many plants that we think of as weeds, such as nettles and dandelions, can be eaten. Prehistoric sites often contain the remains of nuts such as hazel, beechnuts and acorns, and pips from fruits such as blackberries, rose hips, crab apples and strawberries. Prehistoric people who lived in these sites may have had a much more varied diet than we imagine.

### Harpoons

Prehistoric hunters caught fish with deer-antler harpoons, like these found in Yorkshire. Shells and bones found on the beaches of Scotland show that people caught fish and shellfish from the sea. They also ate limpets and sea urchins, which they cooked by boiling or roasting on hot stones.

▼ *A hand axe (1), hand hammer (2), axehead (3), scraper or knife (4), and two arrow heads (5) and pot boiler (6). The stone or pot boiler was heated until red hot and dropped into a pot of liquid to warm it up.*

## The First Farmers

Towards the end of the Stone Age, the first farmers arrived in Britain. Raising animals and growing crops gave people more control over their food supply. Families began to settle in one place. Food became more plentiful and the population grew. These people still hunted – we know this from the beautiful flint arrowheads they made. But most of their meat came from cattle, sheep, goats and pigs. These farm animals were not the same as we have today, although some ancient breeds such as the Scottish Soay sheep can still be found.

The first farmers brought seeds to grow crops. After clearing the land of trees and breaking up the soil, they planted rye, oats, Einkorn and Emmer, which were types of wheat that grew wild in the Middle East. The farmers gathered their seeds at harvest time and crushed them between stones to make a rough kind of flour. Then they mixed the flour with water and patted the mixture into flat cakes. These were then baked on hot stones from the fire.

**Pots and Pot boilers**

New Stone Age farmers used pots to store, cook and serve their food. The marks of bones or seeds, used as decoration, provide clues about the food they ate. Liquids could be heated in the pots by dropping small, red hot stones into them. These were known as pot boilers. This 4,000-year-old pot was found at Mildenhall, Suffolk.

▶ *This 4,000-year-old pot from Suffolk was used for storing food. Similar pots were also used for cooking over a fire.*

## Celtic Food

From about 400 BC Celtic settlers began arriving from mainland
Europe. Their use of bronze and iron brought great
improvements in the cooking of food. Cooking in large iron pots,
called cauldrons, hung from chains over the fire was much faster
for cooking food than using stone pot boilers. Sharp knives
enabled people to cut their meat rather than gnaw at it with their
teeth. According to the writer, Posidonius, Celtic meals consisted
mainly of roasted or boiled meat, particularly beef and pork.

With their meal they drank beer or mead. Mead is a drink made
from honey. Rich Celts as well as drinking beer or mead, could
afford to drink wine imported from abroad with their food.
Other foods they liked to eat were eggs, dairy products, porridge,
wild birds, fish and seaweed.

▲ *A reconstructed Celtic
house showing iron tools
and cooking pots.*

# Roman Food

## A Taste of Luxury

From AD 43, Roman citizens began to arrive in Britain, first as conquering soldiers, then as settlers. They did not care for the simple diet of the Celts. Instead, they brought with them new foods, cooking methods and manners. Before long, many wealthier Britons began to copy Roman ways, and for the next four centuries, their food and cooking was similar to that of the rest of the Roman Empire.

▼ *Jars called **amphorae** were used to carry and store olive oil or wine. They were sealed with stoppers, and designed to be carried one each side of a donkey's back, or put in racks to keep them upright.*

## New Foods

Some foods that the Romans introduced to Britain became permanently established, including pheasants and fallow deer, which still live wild in the countryside today. The Romans were fond of fruit and nuts. They grew grapes (for vinegar) and planted fig, walnut and sweet chestnut trees. To satisfy their taste for strongly flavoured dishes the Romans grew many herbs. Parsley, thyme, sage, mint and garlic are still used today. The Celts lived mainly on meat and cereal foods, but the Romans were fond of vegetables as well. Thanks to them, lettuce, onions, cabbage, carrots and turnips were introduced to Britain.

Some foods that the Romans enjoyed would not grow in Britain's cold climate. But once they had built roads and bigger ships, traders could easily import foods from other parts of the Empire. These included spices such as pepper and ginger from the East, and olive oil from Spain. These foods were carried in wooden barrels or tall pottery storage jars called amphorae.

## The Roman Kitchen

Many Roman homes had a separate room reserved for cooking.
Instead of one huge cauldron hung over a roaring log fire, the
Romans cooked over compact stoves raised on bricks. These
stoves burned wood or charcoal like a modern barbecue. Several
iron pots and bronze saucepans could be heated at the same time,
each holding a different dish. Small ovens baked sweets or
specialities such as stuffed dormice.

▲ *This Roman stove has
a grid over a charcoal fire.
Leaning against the wall is
an amphora for wine and
on the table a mortar for
crushing herbs.*

**Lead Poisoning**

Roman homes often had their water supplied through lead pipes.
Cooking pots were also lined with lead. As a result of lead getting into their
water and food many Romans may have suffered from lead poisoning.
This has the effect of reducing the sense of taste and may explain why the
Romans liked strongly flavoured foods.

## Meals and Meal Times

Romans usually ate three meals a day. *Ientaculum* (breakfast) was a simple meal of bread, fruit and soft cheeses flavoured with herbs. With this, they probably drank goats' milk. At midday, the family gathered together for *prandium* (lunch). This was another light meal of eggs, fish or cold chicken with salads or vegetables. Pizza and pasta, which are eaten regularly in Italy today, were also popular in Ancient Roman homes.

The main meal, *cena* (dinner), was eaten in the evening following bathing. In a wealthy household, *cena* could last for several hours. Guests ate vast quantities of rich food. Every hour or so some guests would retire to the vomitarium. This was a room where they made themselves sick, perhaps by tickling their throats with feathers. They then returned to the feast with an empty stomach, ready to start all over again. However, retiring to a vomitarium was not common practice in most households.

◀ *The guests at this banquet eat their meal reclining on long couches. On the right, a guest who has drunk too much wine is helped from the room.*

*This silver dish was probably used for fruit or sweet dishes. Part of the treasure from Mildenhall in Suffolk, it was buried to keep it safe from raiders.*

**Apicius the Cook**
A Roman called Apicius loved food so much that he wrote down his favourite recipes. He even included some recipes for rich foods such as ostrich, peacock or snails. A simpler one is boiled ham with figs. When the ham is nearly cooked, cuts are made in it and these are filled with honey. Finally, it is covered with pastry and baked in an oven.

Most dinners had three courses. The *gustatio* (supper) would be salads, egg dishes or shellfish. We know that snails were particularly popular from the many snail shells found on Roman house sites. The main course or *fercula*, was cooked meats, fish and vegetables, and beef and pork dishes were more common than lamb. Sheep were kept mainly for their wool and milk. Birds and animals, like pheasant, hare and wild boar, were also popular. Meats were often served with spiced stuffings or rich, sweet and sour sauces. The *mensae secundae* (dessert) consisted of fruits or cakes served with honey.

## Dining in Style

The Roman word for a dining room is *triclinium*. This word gives a clue about how the meal was taken. The guests reclined on low couches around three sides of a table. Food was served, perhaps by slaves, from the fourth side. Knives and spoons were sometimes used, but most people ate with their fingers. Bowls of scented water and white napkins helped them to keep clean whilst eating.

*This mosaic shows servants pouring wine for guests. The Romans brought large quantities of wine from Gaul (modern France), Spain and Italy.*

▲ *A Roman bakery. This carving shows grain being ground into flour and the baker's oven in the background.*

## Food for the Poor

The lavish diet described on the previous page was only enjoyed by rich Romans. Most people made do with a little meat and fish, some vegetables, cheese, bread and oats. A kind of porridge was eaten by the army while it was on the move. The soldiers could make it quickly and cheaply from oats, which were grown throughout the Empire. Once, when the army of the Roman general Julius Caesar was fighting in Gaul (France), the porridge ration ran out, and the soldiers grumbled when they were forced to eat the local cattle instead!

## Roman Bread

For both rich and poor, bread was an essential part of the Roman diet. Even soldiers baked fresh bread every day, using small hand mills to grind the grain into flour. The Romans taught British farmers to grow wheat and barley in larger fields protected from weeds and pests. The best wheat came from the estates of the villas (country houses). It was harvested and ground into flour to bake into bread on site. Sometimes donkeys turned the heavy millstones that ground the flour by walking round all day attached to a wooden pole. The Romans also used water mills for grinding flour. Grain and flour needed storing carefully. Villas, towns and forts, like those along Hadrian's Wall, had large **granaries** to protect the valuable grain from damp and rats.

In towns, people bought loaves of bread from stalls in front of the bakeries.

## Eating Out

Wealthy Romans led a very public life. They often preferred to eat out in restaurants and bars in the towns. These sold wine and hot snacks from pottery jars set into the counters. Even in the country there were roadside shops and stalls selling food for travellers. Not until today has there been such a wide variety of cooked foods available from shops and bars.

**The Colour of Bread**

The bread the poor had to eat was heavy, coarse and dark in colour. The rich, however, preferred white bread made with fine flour. A Roman saying: 'I know the colour of my bread' meant 'I know my place.'

◄ *Roman landowners lived in villas in the countryside. They grew food for themselves and sent produce to markets in nearby towns.*

# Medieval Food

### Lords and Peasants

The Romans left Britain in AD 410 and people soon forgot their exotic foods. The **Anglo-Saxons, Vikings** and **Normans** who invaded and settled in Britain over the following six centuries had no taste for Roman luxuries. Their simple timber-and-thatched homes had a central hearth where they boiled their food in cauldrons over a fire, or gently warmed it in pottery vessels resting in hot ashes. Sometimes they roasted meat on spits in front of the hearth. Later, rich Norman invaders built stone castles and manor houses with fireplaces built under chimneys, but for most people cooking was done over an open fire.

▲ *These peasants reaping wheat are being watched by the Lord's steward who carries a staff and horn. The peasants cut the corn with small sickles to avoid losing any of the precious grain.*

▶ *The cook in Chaucer's book* Canterbury Tales *carries a special hook for hanging cooking pots at different heights over the fire, and for pulling large pieces of meat out of the pot.*

### Self-sufficiency

During the Middle Ages, most villagers had to work part-time on the lord's land. They also had to pay their dues, such as taking their grain to the lord's mill to be ground. Many villagers kept a pig or a few chickens to provide a little extra nourishing foods for their families. Most of their vegetables were grown locally because bulk quantities could not be bought from elsewhere. Only luxury foods such as spices and dried fruits, and one or two essentials such as salt were brought from far away.

## Daily Pottage

Medieval people ate thick soups or stew every day. They called it 'pottage' because it was made in a large pot. It might have been a 'running pottage' like soup, or a 'standing pottage' so thick with grain or pulses that a spoon would have stood upright in it. The rich ate meat or fish pottages, whereas poorer families ate mainly vegetable pottages. Pottages could contain almost anything. One made for King Richard III contained meat broth with ground almonds, minced onions and small birds, and was flavoured with cloves and cinnamon.

▼ *In large households with many mouths to feed, stews or pottages were prepared in enormous iron cooking pots.*

**A Simple Pottage to Make**

Put some bones and chopped stewing beef into three litres of water. Add a chopped onion and salt, and bring to the boil and then simmer for about two hours. Add some chopped cabbage, leeks and celery, and cook until soft. Remove the bones. Thicken with breadcrumbs and season with fresh or dried parsley, sage and thyme. Then serve.

**Warning**

Remember, boiling water can scald; ask an adult to help.

## Fruit and Vegetables

Today, we eat lots of fresh fruit and vegetables which contain the **vitamins** we need to stay healthy. Medieval people did not know about vitamins. They thought that eating raw fruit caused sickness and diarrhoea. They did however eat fresh plums and grapes, but apples and pears were usually boiled or baked with spices. In Medieval Britain, people grew very few vegetables, although they were quite common in the rest of Europe. However, Britons often used garlic, onion and leeks in pottages to add flavour.

*Dishes served at this early fifteenth-century banquet include pies, pastries, small birds and game.*

## Preserving Foods

Most farm animals were slaughtered in the autumn because there was only enough hay to keep a few of the best animals alive over the winter for breeding. Cattle, sheep and goats were slaughtered in October or November. Their meat was then sealed in barrels of salt for eating during the winter. Some meats and fish were hung up in chimneys and smoked. Dried fish, called stockfish, was also common. Food was also pickled, spiced and buried in the ground. A lot of meat must have been rather smelly and unpleasant by the end of winter, so herbs and spices were added during its final cooking to improve the taste and colour of the meat.

*Pigs were slaughtered to provide food over the winter. Some of the meat was smoked over the fire and eaten as bacon or ham later.*

## Meals and Meal Times

A Medieval saying was: 'He that eateth often lyveth a beastly life.' The poor worked very long hours, and had time only to eat small snacks during the day. For the rich, two meals were considered 'sufficient for a real man.' These were dinner, eaten at about 11 am, and supper, eaten at about 4 pm. Dinner was a formal occasion. The lord and his family sat on a raised platform across the end of the hall. Processions of servants brought many sweet and savoury dishes. Important guests were seated at the top table and served individually, while members of the household sat in 'messes' of two or four. They shared food helpings, cups, bowls and 'trenchers' of stale bread which they used as plates.

**Manners Makyth Man**

Upper-class youngsters were often given lessons in table manners, which included:

Do not pick your nose or nails at table.

Do not play with dogs or cats under the table.

Do not remove your hat or lean forward – lice may drop into the food.

Do not hack at your meat 'as field men do'.

Do not put your fingers in your cup or lick the dishes.

Do not 'belch too loud'.

## Fish and Fast Days

In Medieval times the Christian church laid down strict rules about certain foods. Good Friday and a few other days were fast days, when little or no food was eaten. Meat-eating was also banned on Wednesdays, Fridays and Saturdays and during **Lent**. Eating pancakes on Shrove Tuesday goes back to the time when people cleared the eggs and animal fats out of their kitchens just before the start of Lent. Anyone who was caught eating forbidden foods during the forty days of Lent could be punished.

▼ *Fish caught in the sea were difficult to transport, so fish caught in rivers and ponds were also eaten. This scene shows fishmongers selling fish.*

## Daily Fare

The accounts of Medieval households can tell us much about what people ate. In the early 1400s, Dame Alice de Bryene kept a weekly record of all the food eaten in her Suffolk home. Bread was baked every day, white 'manchet' buns for the 'gentlefolk' and brown 'tourte' loaves for the poor. Following the 1266 Assize of Bread, strict rules were made to control the weight, size and price of bread to make sure that people were not cheated by crafty bakers. In Dame Alice's household, fish, especially herrings (fresh, smoked or salted), played a large part in everyone's diet. Beef, bacon and **mutton** were the most common meats. Eggs and dairy products, known as 'white meats', were eaten in the spring and summer, while rabbits and pigeons were eaten in the autumn. In 1413, a New Year feast included 5 piglets, 24 capons (chickens that had been fattened up), 12 geese and 2 swans, as well as beef, veal and mutton. Instead of the usual 40 meals 240 were served!

▼ *Laws were introduced to control the price and quality of bread. These bakers are making small, round white rolls called manchets.*

## Herb Gardens

Large households such as Dame Alice's had a herb garden. Herbs were used to flavour foods, for making medicines and for freshening rooms. Fragrant herbs like rosemary, fennel, mint and garlic, were used for salad dressings. Honey, from beehives in the garden, was used as a sweetner because sugar was very expensive.

**Medieval Cookery Books**
Medieval cookery books were called 'Books of Carving'. Instead of giving recipes, they explained how to 'slat a pike', 'thigh small birds' or 'disfigure a peacock'. After cooking peacocks, they were often redressed in all their feathers before serving.

◀ *This picture shows herbs being gathered by servants, from the raised beds in which they grow. Herbs were used in cooking and in medicines.*

# Tudor and Stuart Food

▲ *Monks had provided free food for the poor. By 1539, after King Henry VIII had closed the monasteries, the poor were left to beg for food.*

## *Plenty and Want*

In 1485 Henry Tudor became the first Tudor king of England. Though the rich nobles kept most of their old privileges and wealth, merchants, craftsmen and farmers began to have more influence. They enjoyed greater prosperity, too. For a time almost everyone had more and better food to eat. Visitors to Britain commented on how well-fed British people were in comparison with other Europeans. It was after about 1550 that things began to change. Rising prices, poor harvests and the enclosure (fencing-in) of common lands on which the poor relied for grazing their animals began to bring hardship. The poor suffered most, and by 1600, many people were reduced to starvation.

## *Tudor Banquets*

The rich dined mainly on meat. In 1533, Lord Exeter entertained King Henry VIII. The first course had fifteen different dishes including stewed sparrows, venison and pear pasties, carp, seagulls and rabbit. The course which followed included more venison, and birds such as stork, gannet and heron, pastries and fritters.

▶ *Queen Elizabeth 1 at a hunting picnic in 1575.*

*▲ An early seventeenth-century kitchen in a wealthy home.*

## Desserts

Desserts were served at the end of the feast. They included fruits and jellies, pies, cheeses and marchpane, a popular sweet dish made with almonds. Many of these dishes would have been decorated with herbs and flowers such as borage, pansies, or marigolds. Queen Elizabeth I, who had a passion for sugar, ate so many sweet dishes that her teeth turned black.

Very fancy dishes, called subtelties, were common features on the table at Tudor banquets. These were sometimes shaped to look like a ship or a hunting scene and painted with real gold. They were often served between the courses as display pieces. Many were made of sugar, but they could also be made from meat. A boar's head or dressed peacock was a favourite subtelty, and appeared often at a banquet.

**A Royal Feast**
When King Henry VIII entertained a 1,000 guests at Greenwich, London, they were seated at the table for seven hours. The final course consisted of twenty different types of jelly made in the shapes of castles and animals. No wonder the king's waist measured 137 cm by the time he was fifty years of age!

## A Law against Gluttony

At banquets, the many dishes shared amongst people did not necessarily mean that everybody ate a great deal. The dishes were shared amongst the messes (groups of two or four) that belonged to a particular group, for example, the household's senior servants. Even though many people did not eat a great deal, in 1541, a law was passed which tried to reduce **gluttony**. Nobles were restricted to seven main dishes, knights and gentlemen to five and other people to four. Soups, salads, eggs, puddings and fruits were not restricted. Even so, the rich disliked such hardship and so largely ignored the law.

▲ *Before the 1560s few houses had chimneys. At this farmhouse, food was cooked over an open fire in the centre of the floor and the diners had no escape from the smoke.*

## Farmhouse Fare

In more modest homes, such as the farmhouse pictured here, the food would have been much simpler. As in earlier times, most of it was grown nearby. The farmer's wife and her daughter or maid looked after the poultry, bees and pigs, made butter, smoked the hams and tended the herb garden. Most meat was still boiled in big cauldrons, although it could be roasted on a spit in front of the fire. Sometimes smaller pots were used to separate different foods. These pots were usually stood in boiling liquid in the cauldron.

▶ *A wealthy family's pleasure garden with orange and lemon trees in pots. In winter they were moved into a glasshouse, or orangery.*

## A Modest Meal

The main meal, dinner, was eaten at midday. The family and guests sat at a table at the top end of the hall, while servants and workers sat at long tables at the lower end of the hall. Both sweet and savoury dishes were placed on the table and people helped themselves to the food in order of seniority. By Tudor times, wooden or pottery plates were replacing medieval bread 'trenchers'. Forks did not come into use until after 1660, and the early ones had just two prongs. For those without forks, knives with pointed blades were used to put food in the mouth.

▲ *All the dishes were served together at the start of the meal. Before eating the meal the family would say grace (a prayer in thanks for the food).*

# Georgian Food

*Feeding the People*

From 1714 to 1830 England was ruled by three kings from the House of Hanover: George I, II and III. Their reigns are known as the Georgian period. During this period, four out of every five people in Britain lived in the countryside. Most of them worked on the land, and raised animals and grew some of their own food. But from about 1750, things began to change as the population started to expand rapidly. More and more people moved to towns and cities where they worked in factories. How were all these extra mouths fed?

## New Farming Methods

Farmers began to experiment with new methods of farming. They improved their land by digging drains and adding fertilizer. They sowed their seeds in rows and **rotated crops** to produce bigger **yields**. New breeds of fatter, stronger animals were developed, and kept through the winter by feeding them root crops such as turnips. All these changes helped to increase both the amount and quality of food available at this time. But the down-side to these changes was that common lands were enclosed with hedges. This meant that the poor could no longer graze their animals, or collect firewood for cooking and heating. In the late eighteenth century there was a great deal of poverty in the countryside.

## The Price of Food

In the early 1700s food was cheap and plentiful, but from 1740 onwards prices began to rise steeply. This was partly because, despite the use of new farming methods, farmers were not able to keep up with the demand for food. A series of very wet summers brought bad harvests, and the cost of wheat soared. By 1796, a loaf of bread cost over a shilling (five pence), more than twice the amount it had been a few years before. Milk, cheese and meat suffered similar rises, and many farm workers who earned only ten shillings a week were unable to feed their families.

### Gin Lane

While food was very expensive, beer and strong spirits were very cheap. It is no wonder that some of the poor drowned their sorrows in gin.
Gin shops drew customers by claiming they could be 'drunk for a penny, blind drunk for two pence.'

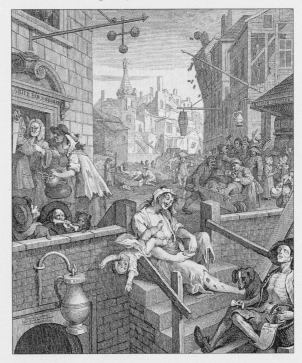

▲ *Gin Lane* by William Hogarth.

◀ *During the 1700s, farmers improved their animals by breeding from the types of animals they wanted. The new breeds they produced were larger, leaner and healthier than earlier types.*

▲ *This cartoon poked fun at the heavy eating and drinking of Georgian men. Too much rich food meant that they suffered from gout and stomach ulcers.*

## Gluttony

While the poor were close to starvation, the rich were more likely to be ill from over-eating. European visitors were amazed at how much meat British people ate. One Frenchman wrote: 'I have known people that never eat any bread while they chew meat by whole mouthfuls.' In 1773, a Scottish doctor wrote: 'In England there are more fat people than in any country of twice the bulk in the world.' Although wealthy ladies ate little to keep themselves fashionably thin, their husbands ate large quantities of rich food. English gentlemen often appear in paintings and cartoons with swollen limbs, bulging cheeks and huge stomachs. Fatness was a desirable sign of health and wealth!

## French Influences

If Englishmen were usually shown as strong and fat, Frenchmen appeared thin, and unhealthy looking. The English blamed the 'unpredictable behaviour' of the French on their diet of delicate dishes and fancy sauces. In 1747 Robert Campbell, a Scottish cookery writer, complained about their 'depraved taste of spoiling a wholesome diet by costly and pernicious sauces and absurd mixtures.' But, curiously, more and more French recipes began to find their way into cookery books. The cooks in rich households began to make sharp and spicy sauces to eat with meat.

▶ *A Frenchman's tea cup is being filled again and again. He does not know the English custom of putting a spoon in his cup to show that he has finished!*

## New Ingredients

The extravagant dishes in cookery books were too expensive for most people. However, some new foods did begin to appear on the table. Vegetables were eaten as **appetizers** or side dishes rather than as part of the main meal. By the 1750s, potatoes were widely available, and many people grew them in their gardens. But they were never a main part of the meal. They were regarded as a delicacy, often eaten 'in their shells' meaning that they were boiled in their skins.

Tea and coffee were also available. Coffee was drunk in town coffee houses, which were like gentlemen's clubs, rather than at home. Tea imported from China became very popular even though it was expensive.

▲ *Coffee houses were popular meeting places in the cities, where men ate, smoked and gossiped over coffee or tea.*

One packet of tea cost as much as some people earned in a week. It was drunk mid-morning and in the afternoon. Following supper, it was taken with bread and butter, cakes and drinks such as brandy and liqueurs. Such was the demand for tea that large amounts were smuggled into the country to avoid paying tax.

## The Georgian Kitchen

Most cooking was done with roasting spits and cauldrons. However, in larger homes new technology was beginning to make the cook's life a little easier. The 'Dutch oven' was a rounded metal shield in which meat could be hung in front of the fire. This helped to cook meat more quickly. Early types of pressure cooker such as 'Pappin's Digestor' cooked puddings and stews quickly by steaming. Coal was sometimes used as fuel instead of wood. This provided more heat and was easier to control. Roasting on a spit was a long process since the meat needed constant turning to avoid it burning. Many Georgians installed clockwork 'spit jacks' to turn the meat automatically. Some even had specially trained dogs that ran in a treadwheel to turn the spit. By the end of the 1700s, the first kitchen ranges with flat hotplates and ovens had been invented.

▼ *This ale house kitchen has the roasting spit turned by a dog in a treadwheel. The large pot on the fire is an early type of pressure cooker.*

▶ *At mealtimes in the eighteenth and early nineteenth centuries, soup was served by the lady of the house and then her husband carved the meat. Guests helped themselves to vegetables from tureens on the table.*

## At Table

James Woodforde, a Norfolk country parson, wrote in detail about the meals he ate. His breakfast and supper, which he ate late at night, were simple meals of cold meats and leftovers. But when he sat down to his dinner in the afternoon he ate several dishes. These might include two or more different meats (roasted, boiled or in meat puddings) as well as vegetables. Fresh and cooked fruits, pastries and tarts were served as a second course. All the dishes were placed in the centre of the table at the start of the meal. Woodforde probably carved the meat for himself and his guests, and a servant then handed it to the other diners. The guests then helped themselves from the dishes nearest to them. Georgian cookery books often contained illustrations showing where to place the dishes on the table.

> **Advice for the Cook**
>
> Jonathan Swift's 'Advice to Servants' (1745) included the following suggestions. They were not meant to be taken seriously!
>
> If a lump of soot falls in the soup, stir it in well to give the soup a high French flavour.
> If dinner is late, put the clock back.
> Always comb your hair over the cooking.
> Do not dirty your towels by wiping the bottoms of plates. The tablecloth will do just as well.

# Victorian Food

### An Industrial Nation

In 1901, by the end of Queen Victoria's reign the British Empire stretched across the world. Four out of five people lived and worked in towns. New machines, scientific discoveries and inventions had affected the lives of everyone.

With so many extra mouths to feed, new methods of producing food had to be found. The building of railways across the country during the 1840s meant that fresh food could be transported from the countryside to the towns much more quickly. Few people grew their own food; factory workers had neither the time to tend gardens or space to keep animals. Instead they relied on shops and markets for their food. Farmers were unable to grow enough wheat to provide bread, and Britain became increasingly dependent on imported foods from abroad. Factory production methods, originally designed for manufactured goods such as cloth and machinery, were also applied to food. By 1900, many foods were processed, cooked and packaged in factories a long way from the homes where they were eaten. Foods such as Heinz baked beans, Bovril, marmalade and Bird's custard powder were common in many people's larders.

▼ *This house belonged to a famous scientist who put in the most up-to-date equipment. In 1878 it became the first house to have electric lights.*

## Cooking Equipment

The kitchen range on the opposite page and cooking **utensils** on this page show some of the benefits of new technology. The range burns coal, which could be transported easily by steam trains. The hotplate makes light work of boiling, stewing and frying. The open front of the range is used for grilling, and the oven is always hot for baking. A turn of the tap provides a supply of hot water. Compared to the large, open fires of earlier times, the range is efficient and clean to use. By the end of the Victorian age most homes had a kitchen range, some townspeople had gas cookers and even electric cookers were becoming available. The toil and drudgery of cooking had gone for ever.

▼ *Victorian kitchens often had new inventions and gadgets designed to save time and effort when cooking.*

Fish kettle

Double or milk saucepan

Boiling pot

### Cow Keeper Shops

Until late Victorian times, much of the milk in towns came from cow keeper shops. Cows were often kept in dirty conditions in these shops which led to the milk becoming infected and many people became ill. Pasteurization, a process in which the milk is heated to kill germs, was introduced in the 1890s. Eventually, milk became safer to drink.

*A cow keeper's shop.* ▶

## Shopping for Food

In early Victorian times, people bought most foods loose. They took bags and baskets to the shops, where goods were weighed or measured in front of them. It was rare to find ready-made foods for sale. Even cakes, biscuits and sauces were all made at home. For some foods, the housekeeper did not even have to go to the market or shops. The butcher, the baker, the greengrocer and the milkman all came to the door every day. Even drinking water was sometimes bought from a water cart since few people had pure wells or a clean, piped water supply.

▲ Victorian grocers sold tinned meats such as corned beef and ox tongue. These were cheaper to buy than fresh meat.

## Manufactured Foods

By the 1890s, shopping was a very different experience. As a result of railway transport, the 'food industry' had been born. A cook's larder might contain almost as many packets, tins and bottles as your kitchen cupboards today. Products like Heinz baked beans, Bird's Custard Powder, Colman's Mustard and Bovril were already household names. Foods that were once expensive were now much cheaper. Flour was produced in steam-powered roller mills so that everyone could afford to buy **refined flour**. From the 1860s, tea was imported from India and its cheapness made it the national drink for everyone. Prime Minister Gladstone even filled his hot water bottle with tea!

◀ By late Victorian times food companies were producing a large variety of **convenience foods**.

## Preserving Foods

Victorian inventors found new solutions to the old problem of how to keep food fresh. Experiments with sealing foods in bottles and metal canisters, or 'cans,' began in the 1820s and in 1847 a meat-canning factory opened in Australia. When the cost of fresh meat in Britain increased in the 1860s as a result of cattle disease, efforts were made to sell canned meats from overseas. But eventually freezing meat proved a better alternative. By the 1880s, the first shipments of frozen meat began to arrive in Britain. Also around this time, wealthy households became able to keep food chilled and to make ice-cream.

**Advert for Allenburys' Foods.** Even babies' diets began to change. From the 1870s, breast feeding became unfashionable and mothers turned instead to artificial baby milks. Unfortunately these milks were often not as good quality as they are today. Glass baby bottles, like the one shown here, were hard to keep clean and some babies caught infections as a result of poor cleaning.

◀ *Allenburys' Foods*

## Victorian Cookery Books

From the 1840s onwards, new cook books appeared in print regularly. Most were aimed at middle-class housewives who were keen to learn new recipes to impress their friends. The best known book was the *Book of Household Management* by a young housewife called Isabella Beeton. It was first published in 1861, and as well as recipes, Mrs Beeton suggested lists of food week by week through the year. She gave tips on presenting grand dinner parties as well as 'plain family dinners'.

◀ *Tips in Mrs Beeton's cookery book included: 'clean as you go, muddle makes more muddle.'*

The up-and-coming Victorian families that Mrs Beeton wrote for employed servants. Without some help it would be almost impossible for someone today to produce a typical Mrs Beeton guest dinner. Even a plain family meal might consist of curried salmon with boiled rice followed by cold lamb, steak and kidney pudding and potatoes, and a dessert of rhubarb tart and custard.

▼ *Victorian dinner parties were grand affairs with many servants waiting at the table.*

## Meals and Manners

Mrs Beeton and her readers were also very concerned about how to behave in 'good' company. These rules were, of course, constantly changing. In earlier times it had been the custom for men to sit at one end of the table and women at the other. But at Victorian dinner parties, men and women sat alternately round the table and the men were expected to engage the women in polite conversation and make sure they were served the dishes they preferred.

## Fashionable Service

The way in which food was served also changed. Instead of two main courses, there were now several courses, each in its turn handed round by servants. This system, called Service à la Russe (Russian style service), meant that each course had its own cutlery and wine glass. At the end of the meal, the ladies went in to the drawing room for coffee leaving the men to smoke, drink port and tell stories.

▼ *At this table, laid for a lavish dinner there are different sets of cutlery for each course.*

### How to Serve Cheese

'The usual mode of serving cheese at good tables is to cut a small quantity into neat square pieces, and to put them into a glass cheese-dish, this dish being handed round... A celebrated **gourmand** remarked that a dinner without cheese is like a woman with one eye.' *Book of Household Management*.

# Twentieth-Century Food

▲ *Up until the 1950s, customers were served by assistants (as in the picture below). Today we take a trolley and choose food for ourselves.*

▼ *This Sainsbury's store in Peckham, London opened in 1931 and had a larger choice of foods than could be found in a small grocer's shop.*

## The Shopping Revolution

Your local high street is probably very different from how it was in the early 1900s. Some of the buildings may still exist, but they probably contain banks and estate agencies instead of small food shops. Food shopping in the 1900s meant visits to grocers, butchers, bakers, fruiterers, fishmongers, confectioners, and tea and coffee merchants. Today, many of these shops have disappeared. Many of us buy our food from a few big supermarkets, often found on the outskirts of towns. Supermarkets offer a wide choice of foods. They are clean and convenient for many people, but for the elderly and for those without a car, getting to a supermarket can be difficult.

## Chain Stores

By the 1920s, many shops belonged to 'chains' of stores such as Sainsburys (founded in 1869) and Liptons (1871). When Jack Cohen opened the first Tesco store in 1947, he began a new style of shopping, the self-service supermarket. Filling a trolley (invented in the USA in 1936) from well-stocked shelves gives customers a feeling of choice and control. Fewer staff are needed and food is bought in large quantities to keep prices low. It is now possible to buy new potatoes or fresh strawberries in midwinter, pasta from Italy, exotic sauces and pre-cooked meals. Supermarkets have changed the British diet for ever.

## The Dream Kitchen

In the early 1900s, small cottages usually had no separate kitchen. A single room was used for cooking, sitting and eating. Town houses had kitchens, but they were dark and small, pokey work-places at the back of the house or even in basements. This was because much cooking was still done by servants. Even as late as after the Second World War, many middle-class housewives did not cook for their families.

It was not until the 1950s that change came about in kitchen design. Kitchens then became light, were painted in bright colours and fitted with easy-to-clean work surfaces instead of separate tables and cupboards. Probably more thought has gone into the design of modern kitchens in the twentieth-century than any other part of the house.

▲ *The easy-to-clean work surfaces and fitted cupboards in this 1950s kitchen made cooking and cleaning easier.*

### Technology in the Kitchen

As the design of kitchens changed, so too did the equipment used in them. Gas cookers were first made in the 1820s, but were not widely available until the 1880s. By 1901, one in three homes with a gas supply had a gas cooker. By 1939, three-quarters of all British

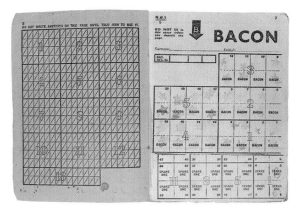

▲ *The butcher stamped this 1942 ration book every time the customer bought her weekly bacon ration.*

families cooked with gas. Housewives were attracted by the ease and cleanliness of gas cookers compared to coal-fired ranges. Electric cookers, available since the 1890s, were not as popular. They were slow, expensive to run and could be dangerous. Not until the 1950s, when electricity supplies reached every part of the countryside, did they become more common. Today, many British families cook by microwave oven. Invented in the 1960s, microwave cookers provide one of the fastest and easiest ways of cooking food.

### Wartime

During the Second World War, food shortages became a reality. During the 1920s and 1930s, British farming was not profitable. Basic foods such as wheat, meat and vegetables were often cheaper to import from abroad than to grow at home. This dependence on imported foods made Britain very vulnerable during the war. The enemy tried to starve Britain into surrender by attacking the convoys of ships that brought food across the Atlantic from the USA and Canada.

▲ *The wartime 'Dig for Victory' campaign encouraged people to grow their own food.*

For their sake –
## GROW YOUR OWN VEGETABLES

## Wartime Rations

In 1940, the government introduced a **rationing** scheme for food. This aimed to share out the available food so that everyone had just enough to be healthy. When buying food people had to hand over their ration books to be marked off by the shopkeeper. Some foods were limited to strict amounts every week. Fifty grams of butter, 4 pints (1.7 litres) of milk, 85 gm of cheese, 100 gm of bacon, 50 gm of tea and one egg were typical weekly amounts. Vegetables and fruit were sold on a 'points' basis. This gave some choice but restricted quantities. Unusual foods such as dried eggs and 'snoek' (dried whale meat) were eaten. While some people grumbled about food rationing, others were glad of their rations. Many people had more and better quality food during the war than ever before. In 1939, one third of British children were undernourished, but by 1945 almost all were adequately fed.

| A Wartime Breakfast Cereal |
|---|
| Cut up some stale bread into small cube shapes. Bake these in the oven until crisp. Add milk and they make a crunchy, nourishing breakfast cereal. |

◄ *In 1936, unemployed men from Jarrow, in north-east England, went on a hunger march to protest to the government in London. They were too poor to feed their families adequately.*

## The Kitchen Front

During the Second World War, the Ministry of Food invented amusing characters like 'Potato Pete', 'Dr Carrot' and the 'Squanderbug' for radio broadcasts to persuade people to eat well and avoid waste. The programme 'Kitchen Front' gave tips and simple recipes. In the 1960s, the elaborate dishes produced by television cooks such as Fanny Cradock became entertaining viewing.

▲ *Fanny Cradock in her television cookery programmes in the 1950s increased people's interest in cooking.*

## International Cuisine

By the 1970s, British food was increasingly influenced by foreign cookery. Supermarkets began to stock foods such as noodles, imported cheeses, soya sauce and pasta. Ready-prepared sauces and complete 'television dinners' could be bought. Eating out also became more popular. Restaurants and 'take-aways' offering Indian, Chinese and Italian foods began to open throughout Britain. Chains of fast-food restaurants such as McDonalds arrived from America and brought hamburgers not only to Britain, but to the rest of the world. With all these influences, it is no longer easy to define the 'typical' British diet.

▶ *In the 1980s many people, after working all day, were unwilling to spend hours preparing food. Fast-food restaurants became very popular because they provided food quickly and cheaply.*

## Healthy Eating

Research into **nutrition** gives us a greater understanding of the food requirements of our bodies. We know that some foods such as milk provide protein and calcium, which help to strengthen our bones, and fresh vegetables provide vitamins, which keep our bodies healthy in many ways. Vitamin C for example, helps the body fight against illnesses and Vitamin A keeps our eyes healthy. We also know that too much sugar can cause tooth decay and too much salt may cause high blood pressure. An increasing number of people are choosing not to eat meat in their diet, something almost unheard of a century ago. Others, known as vegans, choose not to eat any animal products, including milk and eggs. Whatever we choose to eat, we are now more aware of the nutrients our bodies need to stay healthy.

▲ *Children drinking milk at school in 1953. Children were given free milk at school every day until the end of the 1970s.*

**Food Additives**
Over 400 chemicals are available to help food manufacturers keep food fresh or enhance its flavour and colour. Food packets usually identify these by name or an 'E number'. (E stands for European).

# Timeline

| | | | |
|---|---|---|---|
| **3500 BC**<br>First farmers grow crops. | **3000 BC**<br>Hunting becomes less important. | **2000 BC**<br>Bronze tools in use; meat stewed in cauldrons. | **1000 BC**<br>Iron tools in use. |

| | | | | |
|---|---|---|---|---|
| **1066**<br>Normans conquer England.<br><br>Rabbits introduced from Normandy. | **1100**<br>Strict ban on eating meat during Lent. | **1200**<br>Grapes grown in southern Britain. | **1266**<br>Rules made to control the price and quality of bread. | **1290**<br>Oranges and figs imported for the wealthy. |

| | | | | |
|---|---|---|---|---|
| **1600**<br>The Poor Law of 1601 ruled that parishes had to collect money to feed the poor. | **1670**<br>Forks came in to use. | **1750**<br>Potatoes widely eaten. | **1790**<br>Agricultural revolution improves crop growing.<br><br>Kitchen ranges invented. | **1812**<br>First gas cookers. |

| | | | |
|---|---|---|---|
| AD **43**<br>Romans invade Britain.<br><br>New herbs and vegetables introduced; spices imported. | AD **200**<br>Cooking on charcoal stoves.<br><br>Watermills used for grinding flour. | AD **410**<br>Saxons settle in Britain.<br>They introduce cooking on log fires.<br> | AD **800**<br>Cider drunk by Saxons. |
| **1300**<br>'White meats' (dairy products) eaten by the poor. | **1315**<br>Famine kills many of the poor. | **1541**<br>Law to limit gluttony introduced.<br> | **1570**<br>Potatoes arrive in Britain. |
| **1861**<br>*Mrs Beeton's Book of Household Management* published.<br> | **1890**<br>Electric cookers invented. | **1939–45**<br>Food rationing introduced during the Second World War. It lasted until 1953. | **1965**<br>Microwave oven invented. |

# Glossary

**Anglo-Saxons**
Invaders from Denmark and
Germany who from AD 200 settled
in England and Scotland. They were
defeated in 1066 by the Normans.

**Appetizers**
Small amounts of food served
at the start of a meal to increase
the appetite.

**Archaeologists**
People who study history through
digging up sites and examining
human remains.

**Convenience foods**
Foods or complete meals that are
bought because they are easy to
prepare and quick to cook.

**Exotic**
Unusual foods, such as fruits grown
in hot countries.

**Game**
Wild animals and birds, such as
deer and pheasant hunted for food.

**Gluttony**
Overeating.

**Gourmand**
Someone who enjoys eating good
food.

**Granaries**
Buildings where grain crops such as
wheat are stored.

**Lent**
A holy period lasting forty days.
Fasting is often observed during
Lent.

**Medieval**
Description of life during the
Middle Ages (AD 1000–1453).

**Mutton**
Meat from a sheep.

**Nomadic**
Wandering from place to place.

**Normans**
Invaders from Normandy in France
who settled in England in 1066.

**Nutrition**
The intake and breaking down of nourishing materials by the body for growth and repair.

**Prehistoric**
An early historical period in which people did not write. We learn about prehistoric people by studying their bones and things they made.

**Rationing**
Providing fixed amounts of food for people at times when food was scarce.

**Refined flour**
During the milling of flour, the coarse shells of the cereal grains are removed producing a fine flour.

**Rotated crops**
A system where crops are grown in a different field each year.

**Spits**
Turning rods used to roast meat.

**Stone Age**
During this period tools and weapons were made from stone.

**Vikings**
Scandinavian pirates and traders who invaded and settled in parts of England and Scotland (800–1066).

**Vitamins**
Substances in food which are needed to keep the body healthy.

**Yields**
Amounts of food gathered at harvest.

# Books to Read

*Food and Feasts* series
  (Wayland, 1994)

Chrisp, P: Tudors and Stuarts: *Food*
  (Wayland, 1994)

Tames, R: Timelines: *Food*
  (Franklin Watts, 1993)

Ventura, P: *Food Through the Ages*
  (Macdonald Young Books, 1994)

# Index